To Billy Bee,

Engine Number Ten

A Nearly True Tale Told by Rose Ann Woolpert

With illustrations by Jaguar Design Studio

For Bruce, who said, "Yes, I Will."

All Aboard!

Rose Ann Woolpert

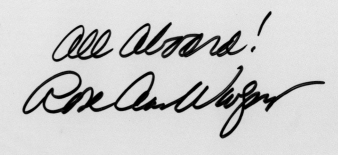

Over one hundred years ago....

at the river's bend near a place called Logan, men used picks and hammers to dig and break hard granite rock for building their houses and roads.

They shoveled the gray granite into small wooden carts, and sturdy mules would push and pull the carts from the rock quarry to the railroad line. The rock was heavy, and the men and mules were very tired at the end of their long day.

One morning, a little black steam engine arrived at the quarry. The man in charge of the quarry asked her, "Will you help us pull these rocks to the railroad line? The men and their mules are tired and need your help." The little engine, whose name was Number One, replied, "Yes, I will!"

She set to work on narrow tracks to carry the rock, traveling back and forth, puffing steam as she went.

Time went by and new roads were built. Another engine arrived at the Logan Quarry and the man in charge asked her, "Will you help Number One to carry her rock?" "Yes, I will!" said Number Two, for that was the second engine's name.

Together they puffed up and down the narrow tracks, pulling little cars with wooden sides. Men loaded the cars with rock and the engines pulled the cars to the railroad line.

More time passed, and people wanted to build a town. Much more rock was needed, so engines **Three** and **Four** and a little steam shovel named Marion came to help. She used her steel bucket to scoop rock into tiny cars, and the engines pulled the cars of rock to the railroad line.

Years came and years went, and even more steam shovels and engines were needed. Engines Five, Six and Seven came to the quarry and carried many, many loads of heavy rock.

Each time they were asked to help, they replied, "Yes, we will! We will help carry rock to the railroad line so people can build new houses and roads." Engines Eight and Nine came too. Finally, the very last steam engine came to the quarry near the river's bend. Her name was Number Ten.

Many more people traveled on the highways and moved to the new towns. More rock was needed, and the steam engines and shovels grew tired and worn. New diesel locomotives arrived to take the place of steam, and the oldest engines no longer carried the heavy rock.

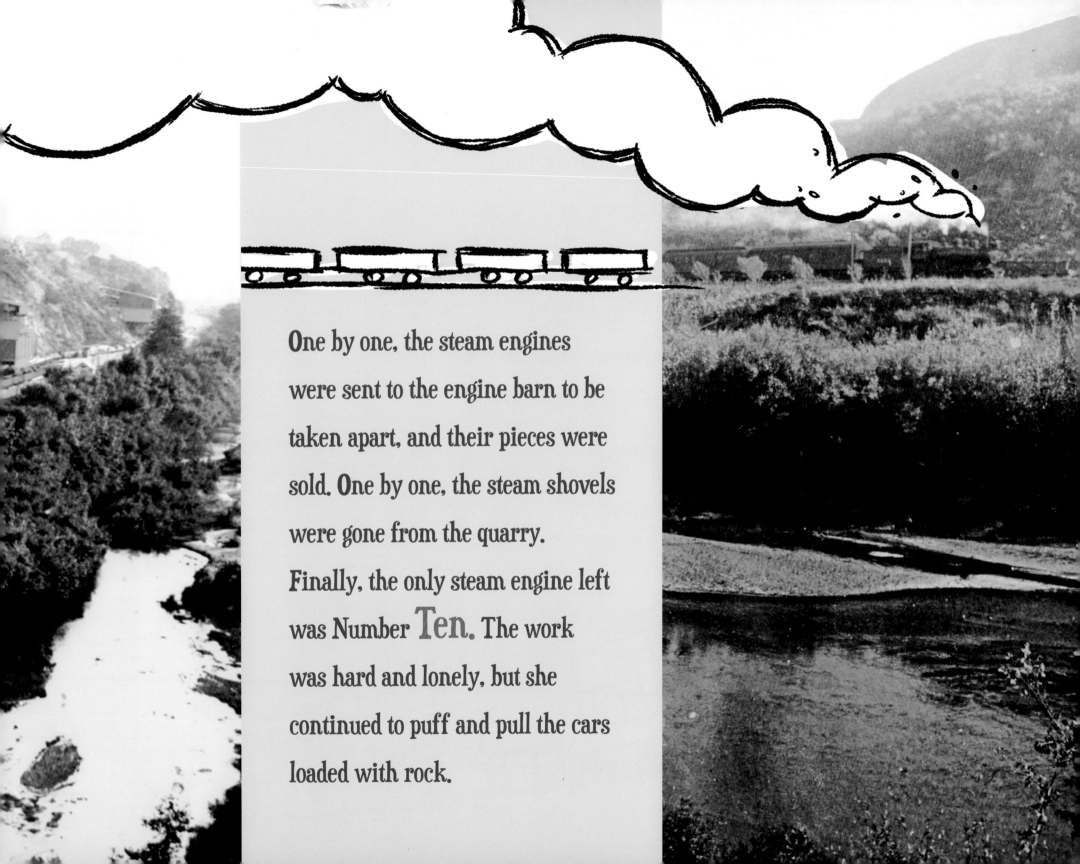

One by one, the steam engines were sent to the engine barn to be taken apart, and their pieces were sold. One by one, the steam shovels were gone from the quarry. Finally, the only steam engine left was Number Ten. The work was hard and lonely, but she continued to puff and pull the cars loaded with rock.

Then one day there was great excitement at the Logan Quarry. A brand new diesel locomotive had arrived from around the bend in the river. The new engine was beautiful, painted bright orange and green, far bigger and stronger than any of the little steam engines who had come before.

When she saw Number Ten, the giant diesel engine said, "Look how old and tired she is. I am modern and young and more powerful than her. I will not need her help to pull the cars loaded with rock. It is time for her to rest." So Number Ten was sent off to the engine barn to be taken apart for scrap.

The new engine went to work pulling giant cars of rock to send to the cities and towns, and everyone admired her strength and beauty. But then something unexpected happened. While hard at work, the diesel engine heard a low rumble begin deep within the mountain.

She heard the
booming voice of the foreman
call, "Look out!" but it was too late, for
the rock was sliding heavy and fast and she could
not escape. Her wheels were trapped and she could not move
forward or back. When the men came to see the damage they asked
themselves, "How will we ever be able to dig her out?"

The man in charge of the quarry had brought his grandson, and the little boy reminded him about Engine Number Ten. Together they went to ask her, "Will you help our beautiful new engine? She is trapped in a rock slide and cannot get out."

"Yes, I will!" said Number Ten, and out she came, one last time, to help set the diesel engine free.

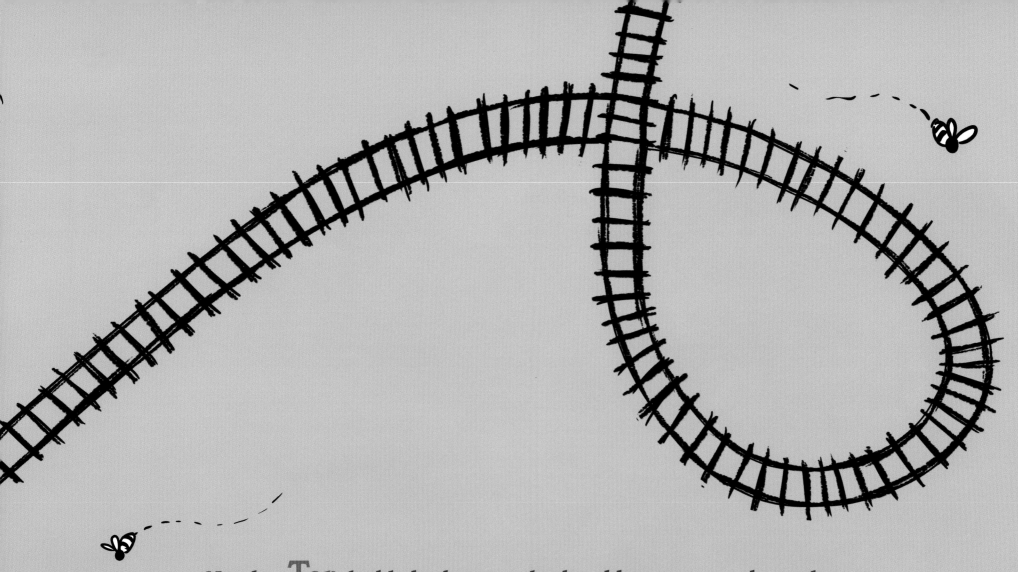

Number Ten had helped to save the diesel locomotive and was the very last of all the steam engines at the quarry, so she was allowed to stay in the engine barn. No one took her apart to sell her for scrap, but many years passed, and Number Ten became very, very old.

Her black iron turned to rusted red, and bees came to live in her cab. In time, the little boy became the man in charge of the quarry and he remembered Number Ten. He came to visit her at the engine barn and was sad to see her so rusted and broken. He thought of how hard she had once worked and wondered if there was a job she could do, even though she was small and rusted and very old.

Then the man had an idea. The train museum in Sacramento wanted an engine to give rides to children. What if Number Ten could be that engine? He asked her, "If we find a new home for the bees and fix you up good as new, will you go to Sacramento to pull railcars full of children who come to visit you?"

"Yes, I will!" said Number Ten, happy to be given a new job to do.

So in time, Number Ten was as good as new, and she traveled from the quarry near the bend in the river to live at the train museum in Sacramento. There she is today, where you may visit her if you like.

You will see how beautifully Number Ten puffs her steam, and how hard she works to carry children from towns and cities all around, who come there riding on the granite roads and highways made from the rock she took to the railroad line many years ago.

The End

Author's Note

This book is based on the true story of Granite Rock Company and the trains used for over a century at its quarry near Aromas, California. Engine Number Ten served with the Army Corps of Engineers during World War II and then worked at Graniterock's Logan Quarry until 1951, when she was replaced with a General Electric 470 horsepower diesel locomotive switch engine.

In 1990, Logan Quarry was renamed for Arthur Roberts Wilson, who founded Granite Rock Company on February 14, 1900, and was the original quarry superintendent. In the 1990s, his grandson, Graniterock CEO Bruce Wilson Woolpert, sent Number Ten to the California State Railroad Museum in Sacramento and had her restored to full working order. She remains at the museum, where she is used to offer visitors steam train rides in Old Sacramento.

Number Ten was featured in Steven Spielberg's 2005 film, Memoirs of a Geisha.